D1405648

Meet my neighbor, the photographer

Marc Crabtree

Author

 Crabtree Publishing Company

www.crabtreebooks.com

Crabtree Publishing Company

Meet my neighbor, the photographer

To John Panjer, my first photography teacher and mentor

Author
Marc Crabtree

Editor
Kathy Middleton

Design
Samantha Crabtree
Margaret Amy Salter

Print coordinator
Katherine Berti

Production coordinator and prepress technician
Margaret Amy Salter

Photographs
Peter Crabtree: pages 20–21
Ricardo Bernardino: back cover, pages 18–19
Roland Guballa: front cover, pages 4–5, 8–9, 10, 11, 14–15, 16–17, 24 (photo studio)
Dimitri Sarantis: title page
Alex Shena: pages 6–7
Shutterstock: pages 3, 24 (all except photo studio)
Ray Stienke: pages 12–13, 22–23

Library and Archives Canada Cataloguing in Publication

Crabtree, Marc
    Meet my neighbor, the photographer / Marc Crabtree.

(Meet my neighbor)
Issued also in electronic format.
ISBN 978-0-7787-0873-5 (bound).--ISBN 978-0-7787-0877-3 (pbk.)

    1. Crabtree, Marc--Juvenile literature. 2. Photographers--Biography--Juvenile literature. 3. Photography--Juvenile literature.
I. Title. II. Series: Crabtree, Marc. Meet my neighbor.

TR140.C73A3 2013   j770.92   C2013-900132-8

Library of Congress Cataloging-in-Publication Data

CIP available at Library of Congress

Crabtree Publishing Company
www.crabtreebooks.com   1-800-387-7650

Printed in Canada/012013/MA20121217

Published in Canada
Crabtree Publishing
616 Welland Ave.
St. Catharines, Ontario
L2M 5V6

Published in the United States
Crabtree Publishing
PMB 59051
350 Fifth Avenue, 59th Floor
New York, New York 10118

Published in the United Kingdom
Crabtree Publishing
Maritime House
Basin Road North, Hove
BN41 1WR

Published in Australia
Crabtree Publishing
3 Charles Street
Coburg North
VIC, 3058

Meet my Neighbor

Contents

4   The photographer

6   Also a teacher

8   The photo studio

10 Taking a portrait

12 Taking students on a field trip

14 Shooting a news event

16 Fixing photos

18 Photographing a wedding

20 Taking photos around the world

22 The next exciting project!

24 Picture glossary

Hello, I am your neighbor, Marc Crabtree. I am a photographer. I take photos of people and events.

I also like to take photos of my family. This is my wife Joanna, and our kids Bonnie and Dexter.

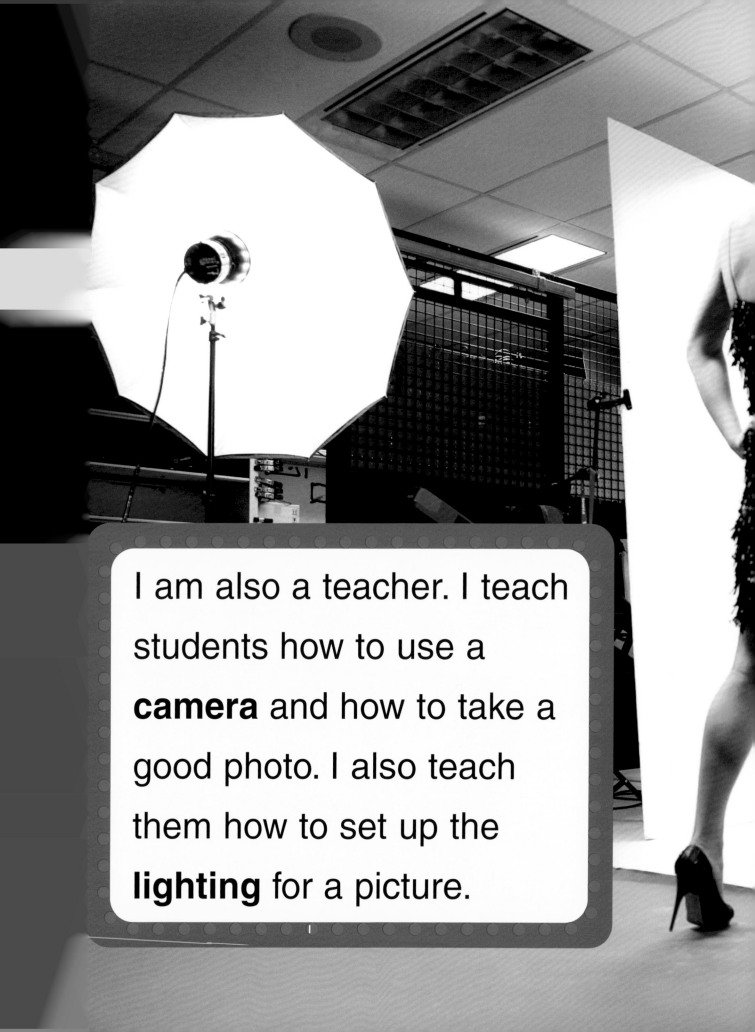

I am also a teacher. I teach students how to use a **camera** and how to take a good photo. I also teach them how to set up the **lighting** for a picture.

I have a **photo studio** where
I take photos. My studio is a
room in my home where I keep
my cameras and other equipment.

I was very busy this week. On Monday, I took a photo of a woman for her business card. A stand called a **tripod** holds my camera steady.

The amount of light in a room is very important when taking photos. I use a special tool to measure it.

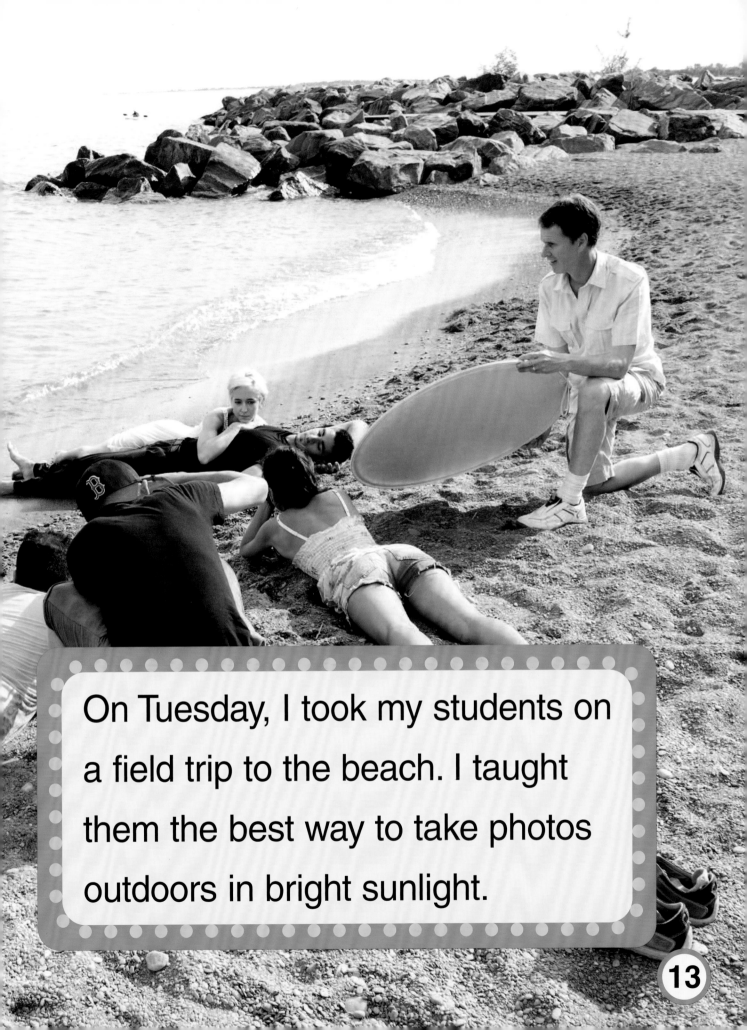

On Tuesday, I took my students on a field trip to the beach. I taught them the best way to take photos outdoors in bright sunlight.

On Wednesday, I took photos of news events for a newspaper. These firefighters are spraying water on a car that was on fire.

On Thursday and Friday, I worked on all the photographs I took during the week. I use a special program on the computer to make changes to the photos to make them look their best.

On Saturday, I took photos of a wedding. For a wedding, I dress up in a suit like a guest.

I took photos of the bride and groom and all the guests at the wedding. Photographs are a great way to remember a special day!

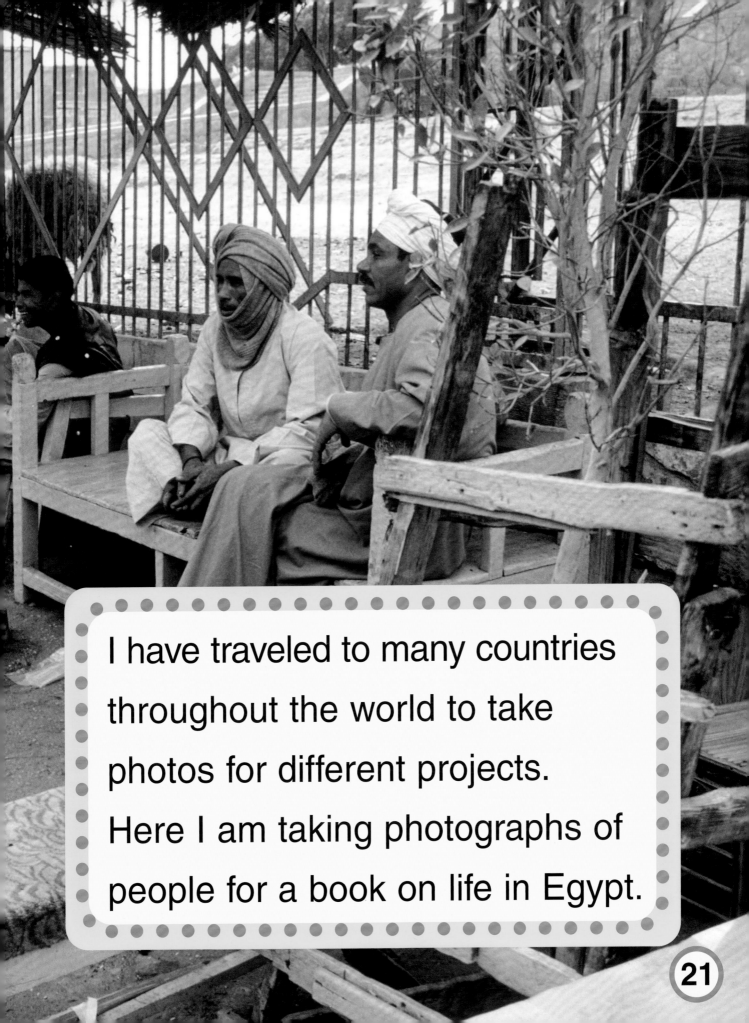

I have traveled to many countries throughout the world to take photos for different projects.

Here I am taking photographs of people for a book on life in Egypt.

My next project will be a lot of fun. I am going on a motorcycle trip across the country with my friends Ray and Greg.

I will be taking photographs of our trip along the way.

Glossary

camera   lighting   tripod

photo studio